UNDERSTANDING
THE
Current
International
Order

Michael J. Mazarr
Miranda Priebe
Andrew Radin
Astrid Stuth Cevallos

Prepared for the Office of the Secretary of Defense
Approved for public release; distribution unlimited

For more information on this publication, visit www.rand.org/t/RR1598

Library of Congress Cataloging-in-Publication Data is available for this publication.
ISBN: 978-0-8330-9570-1

Published by the RAND Corporation, Santa Monica, Calif.
© Copyright 2016 RAND Corporation
RAND® is a registered trademark.

Cover design by Dori Walker.

Support RAND
Make a tax-deductible charitable contribution at
www.rand.org/giving/contribute

www.rand.org

Preface

Since 1945, the United States has pursued its global interests through creating and maintaining international economic institutions, bilateral and regional security organizations, and liberal political norms; these ordering mechanisms are often collectively referred to as the *international order*. In recent years, rising powers have begun to challenge aspects of this order. This report is part of a project, titled "Building a Sustainable International Order," that aims to understand the existing international order, assess current challenges to the order, and recommend future U.S. policies with respect to the order.

The study will produce multiple reports and essays. Three are central to the study's assessment of the international order: One report defines and scopes the order; one examines its status, attempting to create measurable indexes of the order's health; and one examines the perspectives of major countries toward the order. This report is the first of those and reflects the project team's attempt to understand the existing international order, including how U.S. decisionmakers have described and used the order in conducting foreign policy, as well as how academics have assessed the mechanisms by which the order affects state behavior.

This research was sponsored by the Office of the Secretary of Defense's Office of Net Assessment and conducted within the International Security and Defense Policy Center of the RAND National Defense Research Institute, a federally funded research and development center sponsored by the Office of the Secretary of Defense, the

Joint Staff, the Unified Combatant Commands, the Navy, the Marine Corps, the defense agencies, and the defense Intelligence Community.

For more information on the RAND International Security and Defense Policy Center, see www.rand.org/nsrd/ndri/centers/isdp or contact the director (contact information is provided on the web page).

Contents

Figures and Table

Figures

Table

Summary

Since 1945, the United States has pursued its global interests through creating and maintaining international economic institutions, bilateral and regional security organizations, and liberal political norms; these ordering mechanisms are often collectively referred to as the *international order*. In recent years, rising powers have begun to challenge aspects of this order. This report is part of a project, titled "Building a Sustainable International Order," that aims to understand the existing international order, assess current challenges to the order, and recommend future U.S. policies with respect to the order. The report reflects the project team's attempt to understand the existing international order, including how U.S. decisionmakers have described and used the order in conducting foreign policy, as well as how academics have assessed the mechanisms by which the order affects state behavior.

The primary reason that we and others are focusing attention on the international order today is because it is perceived to be at risk— and, by extension, U.S. interests served by the order might also be at risk. An analysis of the character of the post–World War II order points to three broad categories of possible risk:

1. some leading states that see many components of the order as designed to constrain their power and perpetuate U.S. hegemony
2. volatility from failed states or economic crises
3. shifting domestic politics in an era of slow growth and growing inequality.

The order's legitimacy rests on states believing that participation in the order benefits them directly, and this belief is being shaken by various economic and social trends. Any of these three types of threats could prove fatal to the postwar order as we know it.

This report represents the first publication of a two-year RAND Corporation study on the future of the postwar liberal international order. The project as a whole is set to examine three overarching issues: the nature of the order and its measurable effects, risks to the order, and options for U.S. strategy going forward. This report offers a context-setting analysis that defines the concept of international order.

Despite the centrality of order to U.S. postwar grand strategy, the term *order* itself has been used in divergent ways by different observers. There is no consistent, widely understood definition of a rules-based liberal order. This report contributes to the debate by surveying the character of the postwar order, drawing on a wide range of sources, including

- general international relations theory, for specific approaches or claims that bear on the origins and definitions of various forms of order
- histories and treatments of the order-formation process that took place during and after World War II
- scholarly assessments of the liberal order and its possible future
- specific literatures on the causal logic of order, such as economic interdependence, and its effect on state preferences and behavior.

As part of its definitional analysis, the report

- discusses the concept of order in the broadest sense, to distinguish it from the closely related ideas of the international system and international community
- offers a template of the core elements of the postwar liberal order
- defines the U.S. approach to that order and the main purposes to which the United States has put the order.

In addition, the report defines both the general concept of order and the specific liberal international order in existence today. In particular, it explains that the current order is not a monolith. Rather, it is made up of suborders—including economic, security, and political suborders—that have varying breadths of membership, levels of legitimacy, motivating logics, and effects on state behavior. This variation suggests that challenges to the current order are likely to be uneven and that U.S. policy responses will need to be tailored to the specific problems of each suborder.

As the United States considers future policies toward the order, it can draw from lessons about how mechanisms of order have worked in the past. The report summarizes the literature on different pathways by which mechanisms of order have or might affect state behavior. This literature suggests that, in some cases, institutions simply affect rational calculations by lowering transaction costs, while in other cases, U.S. power or widely adopted norms have shaped behavior.

The report discusses the common themes in the U.S. approach to the international order that appear in postwar U.S. national security strategy documents, including

- a rules-based free trade system
- strong alliances and sufficient military capabilities for effective deterrence
- multilateral cooperation and international law to solve truly global problems, such as the nonproliferation of weapons of mass destruction
- the spread of democracy.

As the United States contemplates its future policies, it will need to consider whether and to what extent this historic approach to order will serve U.S. interests going forward. The report lays out several questions about the order that arise from this analysis and that can guide future studies. For example, what forms of order are most important to U.S. interests and international stability; how effective has the postwar order been at promoting U.S. interests, as well as its larger goals; and is the order healthy, and how would we know? Future elements of the study will address such questions.

Acknowledgments

The authors would like to thank participants in the January 14, 2016, workshop "International Order: Framing the Problem"; members of the RAND International Order Study Group; and the two reviewers, Stewart Patrick and Steve Flanagan, for their feedback on earlier drafts of this document. We also thank the Office of Net Assessment for sponsoring this work and providing useful insights into the problems of order.

Abbreviations

EU	European Union
G-20	Group of 20
GATT	General Agreement on Tariffs and Trade
IMF	International Monetary Fund
NATO	North Atlantic Treaty Organization
NSC	National Security Council
NSS	National Security Strategy
UN	United Nations
WTO	World Trade Organization

CHAPTER ONE

The Role of International Order in U.S. Strategy

At the height of the Cold War, a key U.S. national security document argued that Washington should remain committed to the goal of a more ordered international system even in the face of the Soviet challenge. The United States would benefit from the gradual emergence of international institutions, norms, and rules that would stabilize world politics and thus safeguard U.S. interests. "Even if there were no Soviet Union," it argued, the United States would still "face the fact that in a shrinking world the absence of order among nations is becoming less and less tolerable" (Executive Secretary, 1950, p. 34).

This comment appeared in National Security Council (NSC) Report 68 ("NSC-68"), arguably the defining statement of U.S. global containment of the Soviet Union. Even here, in the midst of a hawkish manifesto issued when the world was rapidly dividing into two armed and hostile camps, we find a call for bringing order—rules, norms, institutions, and multilateral cooperation—to the international system.[1] NSC-68's primary focus was on rebuilding U.S. power to deter Soviet aggression, but it was careful to nest this recommendation in a larger concept of order-building. U.S. power and the sinews of international order, it implied, could be mutually reinforcing.

---

[1] NSC-68 further observes, "There is a basic conflict between the idea of freedom under a government of laws, and the idea of slavery under the grim oligarchy of the Kremlin . . . . We must lead in building a successfully functioning political and economic system in the free world. It is only by political affirmation, abroad as well as at home, of our essential values, that we can preserve our own integrity" (Executive Secretary on United States Objectives and Programs for National Security, 1950, pp. 7, 9).

This basic argument—that there is a mutually supportive, and indeed mutually dependent, relationship between U.S. interests and a more robust international order—has been one of the central themes of U.S. national security strategy since World War II. Today, however, there is some evidence that the order itself is under threat and can no longer bear the loads that U.S. strategy has traditionally assigned to it. Some observers particularly doubt whether the leading liberal components of the order, including promoting democracy, defending human rights, and preventing genocide, will survive the transition to a more multipolar international context. The question of whether the post–World War II order can continue to serve as the superstructure for U.S. global strategy is of urgent relevance to scholarship and policy alike.

Risks to the Current Order

The primary reason that we and others are focusing attention on the international order today is because it is perceived to be at risk—and, by extension, U.S. interests served by the order might also be at risk. This is the rationale both for this study and for numerous official and unofficial examinations of the postwar order. The nature and severity of the perceived threats have important implications for the nature of the U.S. policy response.

Recent analyses have catalogued a growing range of threats to the postwar order, from aggressive revisionist powers to regional instability, nationalism, governance challenges, and shifting power balances. "These days," writes Haass (2014, p. 70), "the balance between order and disorder has shifted toward the latter." The most likely future, he believes, is "one in which the current international system gives way to a disorderly one with a larger number of power centers acting with increasing autonomy, paying less heed to U.S. interests and preferences" (Haass, 2014, p. 73). Schweller (2014, p. 1) worries about a general diffusion of power and authority—a rising entropy in the international order. Crocker (2015, pp. 7–8) warns of a "world adrift" characterized by a wobbling international order "in a rudderless transition." The system has become unmoored, he suggests, "because there is an unregulated diffusion of authority, agency and responsibility" (Crocker, 2015, p. 13).

In particular, an analysis of the character of the postwar order points to three broad categories of possible risk:

1. some leading states that see many components of the order as designed to constrain their power and perpetuate U.S. hegemony
2. volatility from failed states or economic crises
3. shifting domestic politics in an era of slow growth and growing inequality.

The order's legitimacy rests on states believing that participation in the order benefits them directly, and this belief is being shaken by various economic and social trends that have produced growing doubts that the current international order is serving the interests of the United States and other liberal democracies. Any of these three types of threats could prove fatal to the postwar order as we know it.

Yet even those who worry about the steadiness of the existing order recognize that it has inherent strengths. All leading nations remain economically interdependent, and their self-interest argues for at least limited cooperation. The group of democracies that has always constituted the core of the modern order continues to cooperate on most international issues. The self-interest of all leading states urges at least coordination, if not cooperation, on shared challenges, from terrorism to climate change. A vibrant United States, Rose (2015, p. 12) has argued, remains "at the center of an ever-expanding liberal order that has outwitted, outplayed, and outlasted every rival for three-quarters of a century." Despite his worries, Crocker (2015, p. 24) admits that "there are more islands of cooperation and joint activity than [the] picture of disorder would suggest." It is therefore unsurprising that the 2015 National Security Strategy concludes, simply, that "strong and sustained American leadership is essential to a rules-based international order that promotes global security and prosperity as well as the dignity and human rights of all peoples" (White House, 2015a). But at a time when revisionist states have challenged parts of that order, U.S.

hegemony is perceived to be waning, and institutions are struggling to respond effectively to non-state actors, the role of order in U.S. national security strategy needs reassessment.

Roadmap and Methodology

This report represents the first publication of a two-year RAND study on the future of the postwar liberal international order. The project as a whole, titled "Building a Sustainable International Order," is set to examine three overarching issues: the nature of the order and its measurable effects, risks to the order, and options for U.S. strategy going forward. This report offers a context-setting analysis that defines the concept of international order.

Despite the centrality of order to U.S. postwar grand strategy, the term *order* itself has been used in divergent ways by different observers. There is no consistent, widely understood definition of a rules-based liberal order. This report contributes to the debate by surveying the character of the postwar order, drawing on a wide range of sources, including

- general international relations theory, for specific approaches or claims that bear on the origins and definitions of various forms of order
- histories and treatments of the order-formation process that took place during and after World War II
- scholarly assessments of the liberal order and its possible future
- specific literatures on mechanisms of order, such as economic interdependence, and their effect on state preferences and behavior.

As part of its definitional analysis, the report:

- discusses the concept of order in the broadest sense, in order to distinguish it from the closely related ideas of the international system and international community

- offers a template of the core elements of the postwar liberal order
- defines the U.S. approach to that order and the main purposes to which the United States has put the order.

Chapter Two defines both the general concept of order and the specific post–World War II liberal international order in existence today. Chapter Three then explains how the international order is the product of five specific engines in the international system, ranging from hardheaded calculation of interest to the emergence of socialized norms. Chapter Four traces common themes in the U.S. approach to the international order that appear in postwar U.S. national security strategy documents. Finally, Chapter Five lays out several questions about the order that arise from this analysis and that can guide future studies.

CHAPTER TWO

Defining the International Order

When discussing policy responses to a fraying international order, the first challenge is to understand what we mean by the term. *Order* has various meanings in the context of international politics, and specific orders can take many forms.[1] For the purposes of this project, we conceive of order as *the body of rules, norms, and institutions that govern relations among the key players in the international environment.*[2] An order is a stable, structured pattern of relationships among states that involves some combination of parts, including emergent norms, rulemaking institutions, and international political organizations or regimes, among others.

The distinguishing characteristic of an order is this settled, structured character: An order is distinguished from chaos, or random relationships, by some degree of pattern and structure. Ikenberry (2001, p. 23) similarly defines an order as a set of "governing arrangements between states, including its fundamental rules, principles, and institutions." The well-established theoretical concepts of institutions and regimes can be constitutive of order but are not synonymous with it. Orders can be built out of combinations of alliances, organizations (formal and informal, official and private), rules and requirements (established by treaty or other means), norms (sometimes emergent and

---

[1] Ikenberry (2011, pp. 12–13) describes three versions of order: order by balance of power among states; order through command of a hegemon; and order by consent. This is similar to the concept of "multiple multilateralisms" (see Carin et al., 2006).

[2] This formulation was offered by study group member Hal Brands.

sometimes calculated), and more; in this study, we refer to these instruments as *ordering mechanisms*.

International order as understood in this way can be distinguished from the *international system*, or the comprehensive global context in which states operate. The international system reflects all aspects of economic, political, social, cultural, ecological, and other forms of interaction that exist among states. The "neorealist" school of international relations theory, for example, suggests that two characteristics of the international system—its anarchic nature and the distribution of power across states (also called the "polarity" of the system)—place constraints on states' behaviors and push them to interact in certain ways (see, for example, Waltz, 1979). These factors can shape behavior, but they are general, emergent characteristics of the system and do not presume the structured pattern of an order.

Some analysts further distinguish between order and the *international community*, which can be seen as "the embodiment of liberal normative ideals exerting an influence on international politics," often through the activities of networked nongovernmental groups (Lindberg, 2014, p. 1). The "English School" of international relations theory places special emphasis on the closely related concept of an *international society*, which forms when a group of states with common interests and values bind themselves together with a set of rules and institutions (see, for example, Bull, 1977). The notion of an international society might presume the existence of an order—indeed, it is difficult to imagine the existence of a society without an order. But the two concepts are analytically distinct.

The term *international order* goes beyond such broadly systemic realities to refer to organized configurations within the international system. Order presumes some degree of institutionalization or established structure—established through ordering mechanisms that play some role in governing the relationships and behaviors among actors in a system. Even if they eventually become quite structured, these patterns can be emergent and unplanned, arising naturally through interactions or planned outcomes. The existence of international order does not presume intentionality or coherence.[3] But it does presume the eventual existence of a structured pattern of relations.

Once in place, however, an order need not exercise decisive, or even dominant, influence on the preferences and behaviors of states. Many variables influence state action, including the shadow of history, ethnic and cultural factors, and the personalities of specific leaders. In this sense, order is one among many factors shaping the ways in which states conceive their identities and interests. Just how important orders may be in doing so is the subject of debate.

From the Concert of Europe to the League of Nations to the postwar liberal order, order has taken many different forms in practice. Order in the sense of patterned relations can be further understood as either an input that can affect state behavior or an outcome of a stable, predictable state of affairs between states, in contrast to disorder or a state of war and violence (see Figure 2.1). Order as input is a structure or pattern created for a specific purpose, to achieve an effect; the rules and norms surrounding the Treaty on the Non-Proliferation of Nuclear Weapons, for example, shape state preferences and, ultimately,

Figure 2.1
Schematic Understanding of the Role of International Order

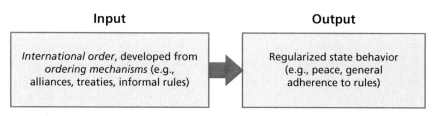

RAND RR1598-3.1

---

[3] Schweller (2001, pp. 169–171) contends that Ikenberry's use of the term *settled* implies intentionality. This distinguishes formal, constitutional orders (such as the postwar liberal variety) from other forms (such as a more emergent balance of power). Ikenberry apparently means *settled* to refer only to agreed or in-use orders, implying that the term could also encompass balance-of-power orders. This debate is of less consequence here than the simple distinction between (1) intentional, institution-based, and rule-based orders aimed at transcending power-based international relations and (2) classic, great-power balancing systems that can be partly settled and ordered.

behavior. In this sense, the mechanisms of order are tools of statecraft. But order also is viewed commonly as a goal or outcome in itself; that is, the ultimate policy goal of using ordering mechanisms is a more ordered international system.

U.S. strategy has understood order in both of these senses. Primarily, the United States has viewed mechanisms of order as tools to achieve narrow U.S. self-interests. At the same time, as Chapter Three describes, many U.S. national security documents make specific reference to a rule-governed international system as a broader goal of U.S. policy.

However, international orders can be built on different sets of values and principles. Major powers may hold competing visions of order—something that may be in evidence more and more in coming years, as rising powers may seek to create alternative (or "counter") orders to the prevailing Western-liberal model. Different value sets derive from distinct political cultures and worldviews and affect the nature of order that states hope to build.

One fundamental distinction in historical conceptions of order has been between primarily power-based, conservative forms of order, which presume a need to moderate clashing interests, and more-liberal versions. Conservative conceptions tend to be modest in their view of how much can be accomplished and for how long. They assume that balances and temporary periods of peace can emerge, but these will not constrain all conflict and will not last forever.

In the modern era, the foundation of international order was built on the bedrock principles of the Westphalian system, which reflected fairly conservative conceptions of order while building on pure balance-of-power politics in order to uphold the equality and territorial inviolability of states. The Westphalian system led to the development of the *territorial integrity norm*, which is the norm against outright military aggression against neighbors to grab land, resources, or people, which was once common in world politics. Inasmuch as deterring major aggression (in such places as Korea and Europe) remains a major purpose of U.S. military power, an order that solidifies boundaries through norms offers a huge advantage.

A more optimistic liberal conception of order—reaching back to Immanuel Kant and Woodrow Wilson but most evident since the mid-1940s—assumes a potential harmony of interests among states and views the instruments of order as mechanisms for cleaning up the marginal barriers to cooperation, such as uncertainty and transaction costs.

On top of the older and more-conservative traditions of order, the United States, United Kingdom, and others have built several levels of sometimes contradictory ordering mechanisms, including a global economic system supported by extensive rules and institutions, a web of security alliances, and a series of environmental and human rights norms that stand in significant tension with the original Westphalian concepts. The result is a "messy, contested and often contradictory bundle of purported rules and expectations" that "does not provide a clean and clear-cut set of principles that can be applied in an objective fashion by world leaders" (Harris, 2015).

In practice, conservative and liberal visions of order—the employment of power and cooperative mechanisms to create patterns of relations among states—are hardly mutually exclusive. Indeed, U.S. strategy after World War II has been based on the view that the strongest orders stem from a combination of the two approaches. Ikenberry referred to the postwar order as a *hegemonic* liberal order for a reason: The United States has used power, as well as idealistic notions of shared interests, to underwrite the rules-based order. In this sense, it employed both hard and soft power to construct the order.

There is an important distinction between the prospect for the postwar liberal international order as we know it and the prospect for any sort of order at all. As suggested earlier, an "order" is merely a form of structured relations among states. Some form of order will almost certainly characterize the international system over the coming decades, but it may take a different form from today's order. For example, such powers as Russia and China have challenged the more-liberal elements of the postwar order (such as promotion of human rights and democracy) but strongly support the conservative elements (such as norms of sovereignty and territorial integrity). One possible future is more-basic global order organized around these principles, with global institutions (such as the United Nations [UN] and the World Bank) placing less emphasis on promoting liberal values. From the standpoint of its national security strategy, the United States inevitably confronts the challenge of which sort of order to seek.

Because order can take so many forms, specific, practical orders are made manifest only at particular moments in history through combinations of ordering mechanisms. As noted earlier, these can include organizations, negotiations, confidence-building measures, organized networks of trade and capital flows, and many other tools. Various combinations of ordering mechanisms could be imagined, each of which would produce different forms of order. This study's focus is the relative value of such orders and relative utility of such mechanisms.

In the most general sense, then, international order refers to patterns of relations that have become established and, to some degree, institutionalized as institutions and practices. Order grows out of the broad character of the international system; it can produce communities and societies but need not do so in any truly meaningful way. Modern international politics has given rise to many different forms of order over the centuries. The version most in evidence today, however, is an elaborate and deeply institutionalized concept of order based on U.S. post–World War II visions for world politics. It is typically referred to as liberal and rules-based. Two dominant questions for U.S. grand strategy going forward are whether this concept of order can or will persist and, if so, what U.S. policies would best promote and employ the order in service of U.S. interests.

The Post–World War II, Rules-Based Liberal Order

The postwar international order is composed of many elements, each mutually reinforcing. Those elements include U.S. power and sponsorship; a set of legitimate global institutions, including the UN and the World Trade Organization (WTO), as well as many issue-specific organizations in such areas as air traffic control, electronic standards, and accounting; a set of international legal conventions, from arms control regimes to the laws of war, that constrain the actions of states; and an emerging set of inchoate but often powerful shared norms.

We tend to equate this version of order with the concept more generally, but it is only one potential variety, and many of its elements are increasingly viewed as illegitimate by countries that believe it reflects U.S. hegemonic interests and power. Nonetheless, when U.S. policymakers and analysts speak today about the international order—and particularly about risks to the order—they typically have this version in mind. The relevant policy question is whether this liberal approach to ordering world politics can survive a more multipolar future.

The postwar version of international order is an especially complex and extensive set of norms, institutions, treaties, and other mechanisms that has been created in service of the following core principles: economic stability, nonaggression, coordinated activity on shared challenges, and the advance of liberal values. Ikenberry has defined the postwar order as a combination of "economic openness, reciprocity, [and] multilateral management," which he refers to as the "organizing arrangements of a distinctly liberal Western order" that reflected larger ambitions than merely countering Soviet power (Ikenberry, 1999, p. 124). Figure 2.2 attempts to capture the operative elements of the liberal order, as well as the primary engines or motive forces behind it.

Within this general framework, the postwar liberal order was grounded most powerfully on two architectures that reflected the order's dominant points of consensus. The first was the trade regime that contributed to the liberalization of global economies and linked the world community together in expanding and deepening networks of interdependence. More than that, the trade consensus stemmed from a core set of democratic trading states whose combined economies were so large that it was effectively impossible to prosper without access to them. This simple belief—that national prosperity requires, rather than merely recommends, participation in the liberal order—has been one of the most powerful engines of the order and its many compromises and areas of cooperation.

The second dominant component of the order has been in the security realm. The functions of this security order were not merely to obstruct large-scale aggression but also to shape the use of force—limiting it, so as not to trigger unnecessary conflict, and enabling it to prevent unchecked aggression or abuse. In so doing, the security

Figure 2.2
Elements and Engines of the Liberal International Order

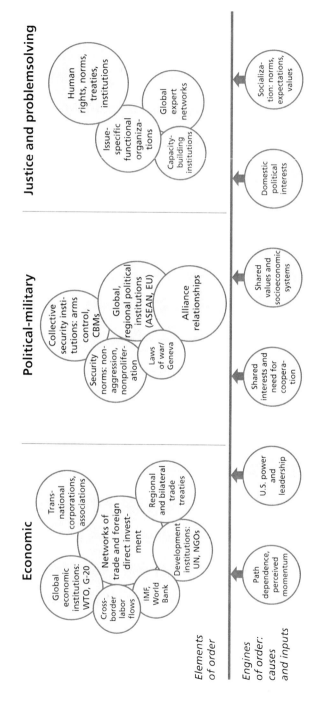

NOTE: Elements include relationships, patterns, networks, norms, values and beliefs, institutions, organizations, and treaties, among others. The "liberal" elements of the order exist across all three components. ASEAN = Association of Southeast Asian Nations; CBM = confidence-building measure; EU = European Union; G-20 = Group of 20; IMF = International Monetary Fund; NGO = nongovernmental organization.

RAND RR1598-2.2

order should incentivize regional and middle powers to follow the "rules of the game," minimizing the use of force as a tool for managing inter-state relations. An effective order also should be able to punish violations of that central rule (Jones and Wright, 2014, p. 4).

The result, as outlined in Figure 2.2, is a broad-based and intersecting set of norms, institutions, organizations, networks, and other mechanisms that reflect two dominant categories (economic and political-military) and a host of other supporting categories and issues. This order has been different from previous ones because of its liberal and institutionalized character. Major issues for U.S. policy today include whether certain components of this order are under threat, which are most resilient, and which might be most important to U.S. interests. Those are the defining questions for the remainder of the study.

The order as it is now understood includes a daunting array of institutions, which generate a massive range of rules, standards, and procedures. These institutions range from the very formal (such as the UN and WTO), which generate official decisions and produce formal records of their work, to more-informal organizations (such as the G-20) or groups (such as the India-Brazil-South Africa group of nations) that provide opportunities for more-private dialogues. Regionally, dozens of forums, such as the North Atlantic Treaty Organization (NATO)-Russia Council and the U.S.-China Strategic and Economic Dialogue, have arisen under the broad rubric of what is generally thought of as the postwar order. These dialogues have many different purposes, from confidence-building to economic coordination, and many different designs.

At the same time, this order was considered liberal for more reasons than its promotion of open trading regimes. The postwar order came to embrace goals of democratization and the protection of human rights, which have become deeply embedded in the U.S. and global vision for order. As Ikenberry, Stewart Patrick, and others have described, this order was not global at first (Ikenberry, 2001). It was initially built within the global democratic community in competition with the Soviet bloc; the order, in that sense, was a strategy for competitive advantage, and it served that role exceptionally well. With the end of the Cold War in 1989, however, the concept of order was extended globally, with the same basic offers: States could participate and be recognized as legitimate members of the order to the extent that they adhered to certain necessary norms and rules.

These other aspects of the order's liberalism, from human rights norms and compacts to calls for good governance, have become integral to the postwar version of order. U.S. conceptions of the order were based, in part, on the assumption that no order would be sustainable if not built on a foundation of democracies with shared values. The order also has offered some degree of procedural fairness, granting opportunities for power-sharing and voice to both small and large states.

A major question now is whether such an order can allow states that do not share liberal values to participate in the order on their own terms. Is the order a sort of buffet, from which states can pick and choose the elements they like and ignore the ones they do not? It appears that Russia, for example, enjoys the opportunity to benefit from global trade and foreign direct investment while ignoring norms on territorial aggression when it sees fit. China aims to benefit from the global economic order without abiding by the spirit of its liberalism in many ways.

Some observers believe that the liberal elements have become firmly ingrained in the overall structure and justification of the order, and it is not clear that they can be easily sacrificed without doing fatal damage to the whole. Reducing the emphasis on the order's liberal elements could begin to pull a thread that would unravel the whole. If states such as Germany, India, Japan, and Turkey came to believe that the order no longer reflected a set of shared values and aspirations for a more equitable, democratic, and open world, their calculations about other components of the order could change. Creating a truly resilient and sustainable order will be exceptionally difficult without the continued leadership of a core set of states with shared values, transparent political systems, and respect for human rights. Once the United States and its key partners in the order begin compromising liberal principles, they may abandon some degree of their leverage to fight illiberal tendencies that are dangerous to the system.

But the dilemma is obvious: The liberalism of the system has been inherently imperialistic, and this expansionism has created some of the order's most notable risks. The liberal character of the order, as Michael Doyle (1999, p. 41) has pointed out, "implies accepting a positive duty to defend other members of the liberal community . . . and to override in some circumstances the domestic sovereignty of states in order to rescue fellow human beings from intolerable oppression." Liberalism thus tends to provoke disputes with illiberal states and movements. The Iraq War, in this sense, was not an insult to the liberal order; rather, it reflected something closer to its apotheosis, and the convergence of neoconservative and liberal interventionist opinions around regime change was a predictable outcome of a liberal order.

This tension has become ever more apparent in recent years, as several prominent illiberal states have intensified their stand against the reach of the order's liberal mandates. Russia and China, in particular, have come to resent key elements of the U.S. conception of postwar order, such as promotion of liberal values and U.S. alliances, viewing them as tools used by the United States to sustain its hegemony. The future of the order will depend to a significant degree on the resolution of this question: Can the leading powers on the world stage settle on enough mechanisms to constitute a meaningful shared order?

The Order in Practice: Complex and Heterogeneous

The literature on international order is surprisingly vague about the specific rules, norms, and institutions that constitute the postwar international order and how these pieces fit together. Indeed, much of the disagreement about the value of the international order for U.S. policy may come down to disagreements about what we actually mean by "order." One way to resolve the confusion might be to think about the international order as a set of overlapping suborders. These suborders, in turn, vary in their characteristics, such as purpose, breadth of membership, depth of commitment, governing logic, and level of legitimacy.

The many institutions, norms, agreements, and other mechanisms that make up today's order vary tremendously in their purposes, breadth (or level of inclusiveness), and depth (or extent of commitments entailed). But the three elements are interrelated. The purpose an institution serves, for instance, often drives the size of membership (its breadth) and the strength of commitments required from members (its depth). For example, after World War II, the United States pursued an exclusive order of like-minded states with shared values to keep peace between its European allies, enhance those allies' prosperity, and, ultimately, balance against the Soviet Union. Similarly, states are generally willing to make deeper commitments to smaller groups of states with closely aligned interests.

Figure 2.3 shows some of this variation during the late Cold War, in 1980. At this time, the UN included most states in the international system,[4] but it was a weak institution whose rules were not consistently enforced. This global order coexisted with geographically smaller orders, such as the Western order, that were made up of such stronger institutions as NATO and the General Agreement on Tariffs and

Figure 2.3
International Order, 1980

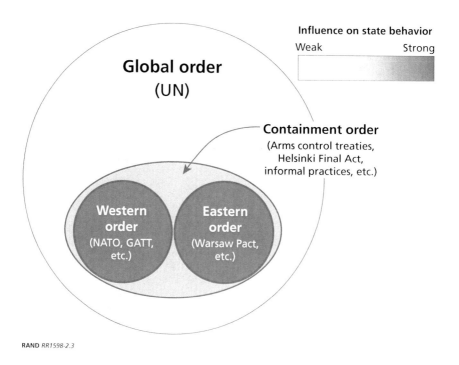

---

[4] Few institutions are purely inclusive—most organizations require states to meet criteria for admission—but some are intentionally designed for broad membership.

Trade (GATT). There was also a separate and competing order, led by the Soviet Union and held together by Communist ideology. By late in the Cold War, the process of détente, arms control treaties, and multilateral negotiations (such as the Helsinki Final Act) had formed a "containment" order, which loosely structured interactions between the Western and Eastern orders.

Since the end of the Cold War, the international order has evolved, but variation in the breadth and depth of suborders remains. The European states have engaged in the deepest order-building by creating the EU and promoting such institutions as the International Criminal Court. One of the most substantial changes since the end of the Cold War has been the geographic expansion of the Western order. For example, many former members of the Warsaw Pact and Soviet Republics have joined NATO. However, this expansion has had its limits. Although NATO has, at various stages, discussed the possibility of integrating Russia, in practice, it has remained an organization whose membership is limited to like-minded democratic governments. Similarly, U.S. bilateral alliances in Asia, rather than a more inclusive security institution, represent the core of the U.S.-led order in Asia. Although Russia and China have permanent seats on the UN Security Council, this arrangement leaves them outside of the core Western security institutions.[5]

In contrast, the United States has been more willing to integrate nondemocratic powers into the economic order. For example, at the end of the Cold War, the United States envisioned slowly integrating the Soviets into the Western order, beginning with such steps as supporting observer status in the GATT for the members of the Soviet Union (White House, 1990, p. 9). Later, the United States advocated for expanding the G-7 to the G-8 to include Russia and soften the blow of NATO expansion (Goldgeier and McFaul, 2003, p. 183). Today, most countries, including most global powers, are part of the core

---

[5]   At the regional level, the Organization for Security Cooperation in Europe is an example of an inclusive organization that brings together most of the states in Europe.

of the free-trading order, the WTO.[6] Such organizations as the IMF and World Bank, as well as such multilateral agreements as the Non-Proliferation Treaty, also have broad, global membership.

There are some concerns that the free trade order could move toward more-exclusive organizations again. Regional trade agreements, which are permissible under the WTO, have been on the rise in recent years. Some have argued that these complement the WTO, offering a way to further liberalize trading policies when the pace of global, consensus-based WTO negotiations is slow. However, there are concerns that powers' pursuit of exclusionary regional trade agreements, such as the Trans-Pacific Partnership, will create trading blocs and spheres of influence, undermine the open global trading system, and give rise to further political competition (see Bhagwati, 2008).

The Order's Governing Logic: Rules or Power

Recent U.S. policy documents have emphasized the importance of rules in governing the current international order. Yet, historically, U.S. leaders have debated the extent to which rules should govern the international order.[7] In practice, there is substantial variation in the extent to which widely agreed-upon rules, rather than power, currently shape the interactions between states.[8] The WTO is closest to the ideal rules-based order that American policy documents (and scholars of the international order) sometimes imagine. There are detailed rules governing trading behavior and a panel for adjudicating disputes over compli-

---

[6] In an important exception, the United States has blocked Iran's accession to the organization.

[7] Ikenberry develops these ideal types in more detail in Ikenberry, 2001, and Ikenberry, 2011.

[8] For example, the Barack Obama administration argued that "our engagement will underpin a just and sustainable international order—just, because it advances mutual interests, protects the rights of all, and holds accountable those who refuse to meet their responsibilities; sustainable because it is based on broadly shared norms and fosters collective action to address common challenges. . . . As we did after World War II, we must pursue a rules-based international system that can advance our own interests by serving mutual interests" (White House, 2010, p. 12). This section draws on Ikenberry's distinction between constitutional and hegemonic orders: When hegemonic power, rather than rules, are at work, states cooperate because of threats and inducements by the dominant state (Ikenberry, 2001, p. 37).

ance. Members of the WTO, including the United States, have high rates of compliance with adverse WTO decisions (Wilson, 2007).[9]

A second important component of the free trade order, the principle of freedom of navigation, operates according to a more mixed logic. The United Nations Convention on the Law of the Sea defines territorial and international waters and outlines states' rights within them. Although the United States is not a signatory, it has committed to complying with most of its provisions. However, the rules of the Convention are not always the final arbiter. For example, China recently rejected a UN tribunal's right to exercise jurisdiction over questions of territorial sovereignty in the South China Sea. The U.S. military has subsequently conducted freedom-of-navigation operations, in part to compel China to pursue negotiations with its neighbors over the issue.

More broadly, the United States has used its power to create much of the postwar order, write the rules in ways that serve its interests, and enforce those rules. Therefore, the presence of rules is not itself an indication that power dynamics are absent. Exploring the variation in the extent to which power and rules operate in different parts of the order may offer insights into which aspects of the order are most likely to be threatened and which might be costliest to uphold as the distribution of power changes. The U.S. effort to use its power to shape the order after World War II was shared and embraced by the core group of Western democracies, which also welcomed the power of U.S. enforcement as their vulnerable societies and economies recovered after the war and faced the threat of Communist expansion. After the end of the Cold War, membership in the postwar institutions expanded beyond the original Western core to include states with much more diverse interests. Today, states with these diverse interests are challenging some of the rules and values that the United States has traditionally promoted within the order. For example, some leading states see World Bank and IMF efforts to promote liberal values and institutions as contrary to their interests and a way to promote U.S., rather than global, interests. States like India, therefore, have sought greater influence over

---

[9]   Simmons (2010) notes that research on the effectiveness of the WTO has been limited by the complexity of the trading rules.

decisionmaking through governance reform to such institutions as the IMF and the UN Security Council.[10]

The postwar order therefore involves elements of both hard and soft power. U.S. military capabilities have underwritten elements of the order from the beginning—especially during the Cold War, and even afterward. But the order also was based from the start on a vision of the future of world politics grounded in assumptions about the appeal and long-term success of certain soft-power values, including liberal economic relations and democracy. A critical aspect of the postwar order is the way in which it has used hard and soft power in mutually reinforcing ways—and an important question for the future is whether the tensions between those aspects are growing.

The Order's Legitimacy: Shared Interests and Governing Processes

Legitimacy can come from the shared interests that the institutions advance or from the process by which decisions are made and disputes are settled. The WTO is an example of an ordering mechanism in which existing and emerging powers generally share the same interest in the continuation of the system. China's rapid economic growth has been fueled by access to the free trade system, and strong domestic constituencies support China's continued participation in this system (Lake, 2014, p. 81; Ikenberry, 2015). In contrast, Russia and China do not see their interests served by other parts of the U.S.-led order. In particular, they see democracy promotion as an attempt to weaken them by destabilizing them internally (see Stent, 2015; Hill and Gaddy, 2013; Buckley, 2013).

Other parts of the order are seen as less legitimate because of the way they are governed. For example, for many years, rising states have called for IMF governance reform, but the U.S. Congress was reluctant to endorse voting reforms at the IMF that would effectively end the

---

[10] Future reports in this series will discuss other powers' views of order in greater detail. For recent Russian and Chinese statements about international order, see Vladimir Putin, "Meeting of the Valdai International Discussion Club," Sochi, Russia: Valdai International Discussion Club, October 24, 2014; "At the 27th Collective Study Session of the CCP Political Bureau; Xi Jinping Stresses the Need to Push Forward the System of Global Governance," *Xinhua*, October 13, 2015.

U.S. veto. Some believe that the long delay in IMF governance reform undermined the organization's legitimacy with developing countries and contributed to the creation of the Asian Infrastructure Investment Bank. This initiative, led by China, could be seen as a small step toward building an alternative order. Recent action by the U.S. Congress to approve IMF reform issues might help in restoring the IMF's legitimacy.[11]

As policymakers look ahead, they could expect that parts of the order that are perceived to be illegitimate, especially by important rising powers, will be the most frequently challenged and the costliest to maintain as the distribution of power changes (Kupchan, 2014). In contrast to challenges to the IMF, the shared interests at the heart of the WTO mean that, as China rises, it is less likely to challenge that part of the order. A significant challenge looking forward is that a more multipolar environment may lead a larger number of states to view elements of the order as illegitimate simply because they serve U.S. interests or reflect U.S. leadership. Legitimacy is not an objective condition, but it is very much in the eye of the observer, and the perceptions underlying these beliefs appear to be shifting to a more critical view of U.S.-led ordering mechanisms.

The Order's Purposes and Its Effects

Once we understand what is meant by order, the next natural question is, what has order achieved? Many powerful variables are working to shape state preferences and behavior, so separating and analyzing a single factor, such as the influence of institutions or norms, can be exceptionally difficult. Although Chapter Four surveys broad concepts of the origins and possible effects of order, the specific question of how much the postwar order has achieved will be taken up by subsequent analyses and reports in this study. But it is important to understand the

---

[11] On congressional approval of IMF reform, see Andrew Mayeda, "Congress Approves IMF Change in Favor of Emerging Markets," *Bloomberg*, December 18, 2015.

debate because it goes to the heart of the potential value of the postwar liberal order.

Given the range of possible orders, it should not be surprising that some observers, particularly realist international relations scholars, have expressed doubt about the effects of modern international institutions (see Betts, 2011). It could be that other factors—the role of dominant U.S. military power, for example, or the conflict-dampening effects of nuclear weapons—have played a larger role in facilitating cooperation through specific institutions or the rise of key norms.

In a larger sense, different theories of order suggest different ways in which it can generate its effects on the system as a whole and on individual state behavior. Some view the institutions or order as tools for *exercising* U.S. power (Posen, 2014; Betts, 2011); others see order primarily as a way of *transcending* power politics.[12] Fundamentally, proponents of these two opposing perspectives disagree about whether the development of strong international rules and institutions serves U.S. interests and about the extent to which potential adversaries should be integrated into the order (see Table 2.1).

The *power-based* logic is premised on a belief that power politics and conflicts of interest cannot be entirely overcome. In this view, mechanisms of order, on the whole, reflect power relationships or facilitate the exercise of power. The power logic expects that rules and institutions will be another venue for power politics rather than a way to transform state relations. For example, a power-based logic can be seen in the U.S. decision not to ratify the Rome Statute of the International Criminal Court out of concern that U.S. adversaries might use the court politically to constrain U.S. foreign policy actions. Although this view does not expect that order can fundamentally alter power dynamics, the power-based logic accepts that mechanisms of order can have a significant benefit to state interests: The order itself can be a useful coordinating mechanism and can be a way of legitimizing the

---

[12] This theme can be found in Woodrow Wilson's proposals for a new order following World War I and in Michael Doyle's (1983, p. 206) description of the liberal idea of a "world peace established by the steady expansion of a separate peace among liberal societies." See also Ikenberry, 2011.

Table 2.1
Alternative Conceptions of Order

Power-Based	Transformational
• Order is a way to integrate with partners and more effectively balance against rivals. Order with adversaries is either consensual and weak or imposed and coercive. • The United States legitimates its power by operating within loosely constraining institutions. • States violate the order when they act contrary to U.S. interests. • The rise of new powers will bring a new international order reflecting the new hegemon's interests, not any objective community or social values.	• Order is a way to transcend power politics and manage relations with all states. • States can develop shared values, and institutions can be widely legitimate. • States violate the order when they act contrary to shared norms and rules. • The order is not simply a reflection of the hegemon's interests, so the rise of new powers is not as disruptive.

exercise of U.S. power to Americans and citizens of partner nations. Those who subscribe to this view might promote one of two versions of order. First, ordering mechanisms could be used to integrate with and establish cooperation among like-minded states to more effectively balance against adversaries, much as the United States did with its allies during the early Cold War. Alternatively, mechanisms of order might be used to facilitate coordination and resolution of disputes between great powers, which was the logic of the Concert of Europe during the 19th century.

In contrast, a *transformational* logic reflects a more liberal vision. It suggests that rules and shared norms can sharply reduce conflicts of interest and power politics between states. In this view, the order can and should integrate more deeply with potential adversaries. By submitting to rules and institutions that meaningfully constrain U.S. freedom of action, the United States can transform relations among states and ultimately serve U.S. interests. As discussed earlier, today, the WTO is the part of the order that most closely embodies this transformational concept. States generally comply with WTO rules, and an arbitration process allows even weak states to hold the strong accountable for violations. A more comprehensive, transformational vision of order would be a global government that includes rules and processes for enforcing them that were largely divorced from the power of each state. This might include an order in which rules were adopted by the UN General Assembly and enforced by a neutral UN court, rather than an order in which such organizations as the UN Security Council grant special status to great powers.

Our project as a whole is designed, in part, to assess such questions—the degree and kinds of effects on state preferences and behavior that the order has had. Those assessments await completion, so this initial report can only highlight the question. For the future of U.S. grand strategy, it is a fundamental issue: To what degree is each element of the order necessary and/or sufficient to promote key U.S. interests? Have economic institutions, such as the WTO, had a critical influence on U.S. and global economic performance? Has the Non-Proliferation Treaty been essential or marginal to discouraging proliferation? In the broadest sense, could the United States achieve much the same results without those components, or even without the concept of international order?

The answer is complicated by the undeniable fact that postwar U.S. grand strategy has committed itself to the achievement of more-predictable and more-peaceful relations among states and to the long-term goal of a stable and value-based international order. U.S. national security strategies have portrayed both the transformative and power-based conceptions of the international order. A change in the role of order in U.S. strategy may produce a fundamental change in the character of that strategic outlook.

Conclusion and Policy Implications

Ultimately, the most important questions about the international order have to do with U.S. strategy and the choices that future administrations will make. Understanding what we mean by order, and what forms it can take, is crucial to addressing these larger questions. Which version of order should future leaders attempt to create—and why? Which set of order-promoting activities should they prioritize? Should a future administration, for example, aim primarily at deepening the bonds among the democratic core and integrating a few significant additional members into the more formal institutions (treaties and alliances) of that selective club? Should it instead prioritize a global vision of coordination on shared challenges?

The temptation, of course, is to pursue all of these objectives at the same time. That broad reach has been a central feature of the liberal international order project since 1945. The United States has built order on many fronts simultaneously, creating a diverse set of ordering mechanisms. It may be the case that this remains the best choice going forward. It may also be the case, however, that this agenda will prove too ambitious, both because of rising constraints on U.S. influence and resources and because of a burgeoning demand from other nations to shape the order on their own terms.

The nature and diversity of the international order has potential implications for policy, including the following:

1. *Order can come in many forms, and U.S. grand strategy may have more options for the future than commonly assumed.* An international system can be ordered along various lines that would promote vital U.S. national interests. Basic Westphalian principles, for example, which are most strongly shared among many leading powers, could continue the norm against territorial aggression.

2. *The origins and structure of order and the shared interests involved point to global trade (and the associated international economic institutions) and the norm of territorial nonaggression as the linchpins of the order.* As argued earlier, the two dominant considerations that led to the construction of the postwar order in the first place were economic and security. The architects of the order were inspired by the tragedy of the 1930s, in which unilateral protectionist measures helped to collapse the global economy and the resulting security dilemmas led to war. In terms of the importance, depth, breadth, and degree of institutionalization of the order, the global and regional mechanisms in these two fields are by far the most notable. The postwar order's leading offer to states is prosperity: Join its trade regimes, play by its economic rules, accept its direct investment, and achieve better

economic growth. One implication for policy may be that attention to the elements of order in trade, economics, and security should dominate the agenda of the United States—as it has for the past several years.

3. *And yet, at the same time, it may be difficult to abandon the liberal elements of the order without doing fatal damage to the whole.* This conclusion is provisional and must wait on further research for a more comprehensive analysis. But the elements of the order built around economic and political liberalization have become so deeply associated with the U.S. postwar project that abandoning or even backing off of these norms could do significant damage to the legitimacy of the order.

4. *The fate of the international order may be disproportionately dependent on the status of great power relations.* As Bruce Jones and Thomas Wright (2014) have argued, "the state of the international order is determined at root by the interactions between the great powers and their capacity to cooperate effectively on the key issues of the day." It is, by now, self-evident that the dominant actor in determining the future of the order, apart from the United States, will be China. If the United States and China can come to some sort of broad agreement on a critical mass of ordering mechanisms, the order is likely to survive to a significant degree. If they cannot, it is far more likely to fragment. The challenge to the U.S.-led order, in this sense, is very different from that during the Cold War. The Soviet Union was an aggressive, authoritarian state whose socioeconomic system was living on borrowed time. Today, however, some challengers, including China, India, and Brazil, represent thriving economies and only slightly distinct socioeconomic alternatives. The potential of one or more of these powers to organize a competing order is much more real.

5. Taken together, the previous two implications suggest another: *The United States may face an increasingly urgent choice between the order's depth and breadth.* The liberalism of the order is increasingly in tension with its reach. Key states, such as China, Russia, and even Brazil and Turkey, have growing issues with

liberal principles that demand violation of state sovereignty to promote certain values. The central dilemma in U.S. policy toward the order may be that responding to the risks demands both greater enforcement of key norms and a more inclusive and at times relaxed approach to those same norms in order to sustain the support of leading states. The ultimate question is whether the order will be most in danger by alienating major powers or by narrowing its focus.

6. *The relationship among parts of the order may become even more difficult to understand and assess.* Today, choices regarding one part of the order (such as trade) are likely to affect other parts (such as security cooperation). These effects can be indirect and hard to grasp. The complexity of the order's relationships is likely to grow as it becomes even more diverse. One implication may be that it becomes even more difficult to anticipate how any given policy choice will affect the order.

7. *As a result, there is no simple, linear way to enhance the post-war order.* Any approach to sustaining or deepening this order must grapple with numerous potential institutions, norms, and tools. The toughest challenge for U.S. policy, in fact, may be to manage the multiple dilemmas and tensions that arise among distinct parts of the order. As the order continues to become more diverse and as a larger number of states seek to influence its rules, the United States is likely to have to prioritize in its efforts to sustain elements of the order. It will need criteria to make this judgment, such as which components of the order benefit U.S. interests the most and which remain feasible.

Engines of International Order

The United States and other sponsors of international order have employed many instruments to advance such order. An important question for the future of U.S. policy is how to prioritize U.S. efforts toward international order. In particular, why should the United States invest in ordering mechanisms, and how much and in which mechanisms should it invest? To make those judgments, it is helpful to understand which types of ordering mechanisms have the greatest chance to affect behavior.[1] In some cases, there remains a substantial debate about the significance of parts of the postwar order in shaping state preferences and behavior.

This chapter seeks to inform that discussion by laying out broad theories of the origins and effects of order.[2] This does not represent direct evidence for the value of elements of the postwar order, but rather offers a framework for evaluating potential effects. It outlines five concepts of the basic causal mechanisms by which ordering mechanisms may influence the behavior of state and non-state actors (see

---

[1] As Axelrod and Keohane (1986, p. 252) note, "The question is under what conditions international institutions—broadly defined as 'recognized patterns of practice around which expectations converge'—facilitate significant amounts of cooperation for a period of time. Clearly, such institutions can change the incentives for countries affected by them, and can in turn affect the strategic choices governments make in their own self-interest."

[2] From a theoretical standpoint, the concepts of order, institutions, regimes, and ordering mechanisms overlap significantly. Therefore, they are treated together in this section. For an overview of how these terms have been used in the literature over time, see Wilson, 2012, pp. 570–573.

Figure 3.1). It concludes by offering a framework designed to evaluate when ordering mechanisms are likely to be most influential. This analysis is designed to help understand how international orders can generate outcomes.

Rational Pursuit of Common Interests

Rationalist theories explain the emergence and success of elements of international order as the result of conscious coordination efforts. States intentionally create ordering mechanisms to achieve specific common interests, objectives which they would be less likely to achieve efficiently, or at all, in the absence of an ordering mechanism (Koremenos, Lipson, and Snidal, 2001; see also Haggard and Simmons, 1987, p. 492; Martin and Simmons, 1998, pp. 735, 744).[3] In an interdependent system, states' interests naturally overlap; networked and shared fates produce a need for ordering mechanisms. But because such barriers as lack of trust and concern for relative gains can impede states' ability to achieve their common interests, states create rules, norms, and institutions to facilitate cooperation, particularly in issue areas

Figure 3.1
Role of Causal Mechanisms

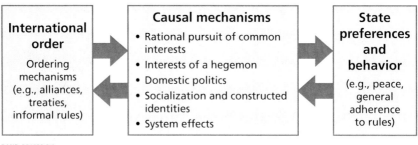

RAND RR1598-3.1

---

[3] These theories hold, in part, that "states construct and shape institutions to advance their goals" (Koremenos, Lipson, and Snidal, 2001).

that are relatively apolitical and positive-sum and that involve repeated, reciprocal interactions between states (Weiss, 2015, p. 1222).[4]

Many components of the postwar order reflect rationalist influences. For example, to counter piracy, states with shared interests in commerce have built an international legal foundation and coordinating institutions (Roach, 2010). Several global governance institutions that reflect shared interests exercise significant independent authority in their areas; examples include the International Civil Aviation Organization and the World Bank.[5]

A review of the relevant literature suggests that, in the view of rationalist theories, ordering mechanisms catalyze cooperation primarily by

- reducing the transaction costs by creating established channels for interaction
- defining coordination points where collaboration can occur (Martin and Simmons, 1998, p. 745)
- building physical capabilities to tackle problems (e.g., peacekeeping)[6]

---

[4] In recent years, this is perhaps best exemplified by Keohane's "rationalist-functionalist" approach to collaboration against coordination problems. Some scholars have pointed to the Concert of Europe as a classic historical case of rationalist commitment to a form of order. The Concert emerged from "the common realization of European statesmen of the Napoleonic era that something new and different must be devised to mitigate the increasingly chaotic and warlike balance-of-power system of the previous century" (Elrod, 1976, pp. 161, 168–169; see also Schroeder, 1986, pp. 2, 4, 9, 11, 12).

[5] As with each of these theoretical traditions, the area of rationalist cooperation has been subject to critiques. Concern for relative gains, some argue, can obstruct collaboration. The strongly felt need to cooperate is temporary and often tied to end-of-war lessons; as memory fades, concert systems decay (Jervis, 1986, p. 61). Some orders can be fragile, and states see opportunities to cheat or leave. And when key individual leaders lose faith in these systems, they tend to collapse. After 1848, for example, European leaders faced an increasing "temptation to play fast and loose with the rules of the game" and leaders "failed to exercise self-restraint and refused to honor the rules of the Concert," particularly in the period leading up to the Crimean War (Elrod, 1976, p. 172). "Most simply, . . . concert diplomacy broke down because statesmen refused to abide by its rules—and they did not give much thought to what rules of international politics they would prefer as a substitute" (Elrod, 1976, p. 173).

[6] On the value of such institutions, see Crocker, 2015, pp. 14–15.

- creating mechanisms to share, vet, and evaluate information (Krasner, 1982, p. 504)
- generating an expectation of reciprocity[7]
- empowering democracies to find avenues to cooperation (Hasenclever and Weiffen, 2006)
- developing and publicizing ideas for solving problems (Weiss, 2015, pp. 1226–1229)[8]
- resolving states' uncertainties about one another by signaling intentions (Kydd, 2000)
- enhancing the "shadow of the future" by institutionalizing the time horizons and stakes involved in issues (Axelrod and Keohane, 1986, p. 232).

If rationalist cooperation explanations for order are valid, the literature suggests that ordering mechanisms are likely to have the greatest positive effect on issues when the benefits

- far outweigh the costs of membership or participation in the ordering mechanisms
- address issues that are relatively apolitical and technocratic; in other words, when states are not concerned about relative gains
- build on established mechanisms, procedures, or tools that have well-developed processes, relationships, and trust
- help states justify difficult short-term decisions by placing them into the context of future interests
- are established among democracies
- reflect voluntary procedures rather than demanding coercive enforcement of rules.

---

[7] According to Axelrod and Keohane (1986, p. 249), regimes do not substitute for fundamental perception of reciprocity but can "reinforce and institutionalize it"; they also can "delegitimize defection and thereby make it more costly" (p. 250).

[8] For example, Weiss writes that, as a "norm- and standard-setter," the UN has promulgated key ideas about order, promoted them, created systems for monitoring, and acted as the ghost of enforcement.

Interests of a Hegemonic Power

A second broad causal explanation for the link between order and behavior emphasizes the role of a hegemon in sponsoring and enforcing an international system. The hegemon—often explicitly—imposes its vision for the international system on less-powerful states by creating ordering mechanisms that help it achieve its interests, often less expensively than it could in the absence of such mechanisms. That power can be more or less legitimate, but any meaningful order will reflect the power and interests of the hegemon or a small number of leading powers (Keohane, 2002, p. 31; Chorev and Babb, 2009; Ikenberry, 2011, pp. 55–57, 60–62).

There is abundant evidence that many ordering mechanisms in the postwar order reflect the influence of U.S. power. The order's entire superstructure was created in service of the U.S. vision of a peaceful, liberal trading system. Specific mechanisms, such as economic institutions and regional alliances, were proposed, shaped, funded, and, in some cases, enforced by a powerful United States.[9]

These theories argue that ordering mechanisms help the hegemon achieve its interests primarily by

- offering the hegemon processes and avenues to promote its interests by writing or strongly influencing organizational charters, rules, and norms that will govern the system
- legitimizing the hegemon's power by creating a shared investment in the order
- transferring some responsibilities for maintaining the order to others.

---

[9] This model does not do a good job of explaining institutions and cooperation that arise independent of the U.S. role. Such a model might be unsustainable. Institutions with universally applicable rules and more opportunities for smaller players are more likely to be sustainable (Snyder, 2013, p. 214).

If hegemonic explanations for order are valid, the relevant literature suggests that ordering mechanisms are likely to have the greatest positive effect on issues when

- the hegemonic power sees a need or opportunity to establish rules, norms, or institutions on a particular issue to achieve its interests more efficiently
- the power of the hegemon is most undisputed
- the hegemon's proposed ordering vision is widely shared.

Domestic Politics

Domestic interests within key states can drive a state's participation in the order (see Haggard and Simmons, 1987, pp. 499, 515–517). These groups can seek order for specific instrumental or ideological reasons: Some need rules or norms to establish a stable context for their goals and to advance their interests (Martin and Simmons, 1998, pp. 732, 735); others favor order as a component of their worldview (Krasner, 1982, pp. 505, 507; Moravscik, 1997, p. 537).[10] This approach would suggest that changes in the balance of power among domestic interest groups will alter a state's engagement with order. In particular, nongovernmental interest groups can use ordering mechanisms to gain leverage.

Some components of the postwar order clearly reflect an intersection between domestic interests and mechanisms of order (Cortell and Davis, 1996). For example, interest groups have played critical roles in shaping mechanisms for climate and human rights policies, both by pressuring their own governments and by working to generate independent ideas.[11]

---

[10] For an EU-specific analysis of this model, see Walsh, 2001.

[11] Like the other models characterizing the origins of order, the domestic politics explanation suffers from potential flaws. It has difficulty accounting for several strategies toward order that seem clearly a product of state-level rationalist preferences. The mechanism of influence can be somewhat indirect and ambiguous. Given differing views among such actors, there would presumably be a wide and confusing array of attitudes and policies toward order, both in general and on specific issues, but how these are resolved into a choice is not clear.

According to this view, states are more likely to participate in components of the international order when those ordering mechanisms

- create the basis for coordinated action—by exchanging information, lowering transaction costs, and much more—on issues of concern to domestic groups
- provide mechanisms for domestic groups to gain leverage on the state's laws or norms, or provide an avenue for rallying global standards to bolster its arguments
- reflect the worldviews and interests of some domestic interests
- provide venues for interest groups to build consensus and propose agendas
- do not contradict the goals or beliefs of many such interest groups
- involve issues that reflect basic preference aggregation through coordinated action, especially on relatively apolitical or technocratic issues
- deal with issues on which there are limited agreed-upon preferences at the state level or that are of secondary importance to state leadership.

Socialization and Constructed Identities

A fourth approach to understanding the actual and potential effects of international order directs our attention to the role of socialized norms, beliefs, and shared understandings in shaping behavior. In their more limited version, these theories constitute a sort of "upper end" of rationalist approaches—self-interested interactions with some degree of socialization, which create self-sustaining processes of mutual identity formation.[12] At the more elaborate end of the spectrum, theories of socialization suggest avenues to more fully internalized beliefs, values, and norms. Identities and interests change "through continued interaction" (Snyder, 2013, pp. 211–212; Finnemore, 1993). This can happen,

---

[12] The English School's discussion of a transition from international system to aspects of international society reflects some of this spirit. The theory would seem to argue that instrumental interaction inevitably takes on a social construct (Buzan, 1993, pp. 330–335).

in part, through the activities of an international community of non-governmental actors operating on the basis of and working to promote shared norms and values (Lindberg, 2014, p. 15).[13]

The postwar order has seen the effect of the socialization model on a wide range of issues.[14] International human rights practices have become more internalized—especially in the democracies, but even beyond. In security terms, the idea of a territorial integrity norm has arguably been thoroughly socialized in national leaderships; the question is whether occasional violations prove the norm by exception. Some scholars have emphasized the role of socialization in international law.[15]

According to this view, states are more likely to participate in ordering mechanisms when

- a recent conflict or crisis, or a perceived need to restore or enhance legitimacy, has created the opportunity to restructure norms and relations (Ikenberry and Kupchan, 1990)
- sufficient time has passed to allow for the emergence of constructed norms and beliefs
- norms have been shared and socialized among elites
- proposed norms have high prominence and an active entrepreneur (Florini, 1996)
- the normative consensus on an issue is the strongest (Nadelmann, 1990)

---

[13] Lindberg argues that, while such an informal international community is a nonofficial plea for what world politics can be, it is not merely theoretical; it is an "aspiration whose avatar can and does appeal in the world, in various forms, and actually does influence politics among nations" (Lindberg, 2014, p. 15).

[14] This theory also faces potential problems and criticisms. The processes by which socialization and internalization occur, at least in the context of international relations, tend to be undertheorized. Socialized norms themselves have questionable strength and have not been proven to withstand instrumentalist or ideological challenge. Attitudes can change, and what has been socialized at one time could be abandoned later.

[15] See Koh, 1996–1997, which argues, "As transnational actors interact, they create patterns of behavior that ripen into institutions, regimes, and transnational networks" (Koh, 1996–1997, p. 2654). These interactions produce norms, which become internalized in domestic law and fully "enmeshed" with international legal regimes.

- the groups of states discussing issues already share values; it is when the underlying norms are most "taken for granted" that socialization can have its greatest effect (Hawkins, 2004)
- the issues have a high-value content and informational uncertainty or involve subjects of human security (Keck and Sikkink, 1999)
- the groups of states are smaller in number and have a higher degree of interaction, such as in regional (as opposed to global) organizations (Pevehouse, 2002).

Systemic Effects

Systemic effects in an interactive system of states can drive states' participation in the order. One such systemic effect is the attractive force of the global economy: There is simply no meaningful route to sustainable prosperity outside the scope of the interdependent global market (Snyder, 2013, p. 210). This creates the "golden handcuffs" effect, which increases the premium on membership in the system.

A second systemic effect comes from increasing returns and path dependence (Ikenberry, 2011, pp. 46, 67–68, 71–75; Pierson, 2000).[16] There is a self-reinforcing effect of ordering mechanisms, and when states that succeed in solving problems on one issue build the confidence to solve other problems, effects may spill over to other issues (Pierson, 2000, p. 256; see also Snyder, 2013, pp. 230–231).

Third, a system of regular interactions can drive participation in ordering mechanisms by intensifying the desire for recognition, a specific form of socialized norm. Mutual respect and membership in collective bodies are keys to prestige, reputation, social influence, and domestic and international legitimacy (Keohane, 2002, p. 8; Larson and Shevchenko, 2010). Regimes and institutions can "help to facili-

---

[16] On the lock-in and binding effects of institutions, see Ikenberry, 2011, pp. 67–68; Martin and Simmons, 1998, p. 746; and Krasner, 1982, p. 500.

tate cooperation by making it both easier and more desirable to acquire a good reputation" (Axelrod and Keohane, 1982, p. 250).[17]

Systemic effects appear to have played a significant role in encouraging states to participate in the postwar international order, thereby spurring its rise. The requirement to remain part of a networked global economy may be the single greatest engine of orderly behavior, both within the economic sphere and beyond it. The price of being "thrown out of the club" is simply too high for most states to accept. The desire for mutual recognition also seems to have driven many states to join international institutions. There is some evidence of path dependency in the formation of ordering mechanisms.[18]

Systemic theories suggest that states are most likely to participate in ordering mechanisms when

- those ordering mechanisms emerge in such areas as trade, and states thus feel unable to remain aloof from the order
- recognition goals are especially powerful—for example, on issues of high global political salience, where being left out is especially insulting
- increasing returns are most in evidence—arguably in global economic institutions, for example
- the issues involved are mostly apolitical and technocratic, allowing these abstract systemic effects to work free of political constraint
- nongovernmental "shaming" activities that use a state's desire for reputation as leverage are combined with pressure from domestic interests and third-party states and institutions.

---

[17] The other side of this coin is the urge to avoid stigma or a perception of deviance from international norms.

[18] Some empirical evidence suggests that order actually produces a *divergence* effect, because states within institutions grow closer and those outside the order move even further away (Martin and Simmons, 1998, pp. 754–755). In addition, path dependence does not necessarily imply stability. Instead, it can exacerbate complex adaptive effects; small shifts early on in the process can send the system into wildly divergent directions (Pierson, 2000, p. 253).

Conclusion and Policy Implications

This roster of theories of the origins and effects of order can be used to support many specific policy recommendations. As a spur to discussion, we propose the following hypotheses that appear to flow from the findings in this chapter:

1. *Order is easiest to create and has its greatest effects among states that share significant norms and values—specifically, the global community of democracies.*[19] This points in the direction of policy options that build from the base of democracies outward.

2. *The factors impelling the growth and success of order will be much more powerful in trade, finance, and economics than in other areas.* Shared interests, systemic effects gathering states together, and other factors are strongest here. One potential challenge is that the existing economic order is a function of U.S. hegemonic power; if several states abandon its liberal assumptions for a different economic order, the perceived value of the existing order could ebb. But this empirical finding does suggest that efforts to sustain the order could be grounded in such institutions as the WTO, IMF, and World Bank.

3. *Efforts to sustain order can begin and be grounded in expanded efforts on apolitical and technocratic issues (e.g., standardization of weights and measures),* which allow the most room for easy coordination.

4. *Strategies for order preservation on specific issues should employ several mutually reinforcing factors: shared interests, the role of domestic interest groups, U.S. leadership, and the risks of refusal to participate.* Ordering mechanisms work best when they reflect the combined efforts of many supporting variables. In the case

---

[19] Lindberg (2014, p. 14) argues that an international community has the most effect on behavior when actions on its behalf possess a "strong[ly] articulated and widely accepted moral justification beyond the national interests of the states involved" on issues where there is "a baseline of substantive agreement on normative matters." He therefore argues that the most appropriate policy-relevant applications of international community are those focused on the most deeply shared norms.

of environmental issues, for example, an overall order-building agenda could combine the role of domestic environmental groups, the role of existing institutions (such as the UN) to give the cause legitimacy, analysis and communication to clarify shared interests, and new institutions to socialize norms.

5. *Order can either fragment or deepen in the wake of catalytic events, which should be used as opportunities for reinforcing rather than weakening the factors supporting order.* In the wake of the terrorist attacks on September 11, 2001, for example, global regimes on counterterrorism became stronger, even as damage was done to other areas of consensus by excessive unilateral U.S. behavior. U.S. policymakers should be on the lookout for future events that offer opportunities to deepen the order.

6. *The United States should actively seek public-private alliances to promote ordering mechanisms.* Often, the greatest progress can be made when several lines of state and non-state efforts coalesce.

7. *The United States should make more-concerted efforts to sustain and deepen global networks of policy elites.* Ordering mechanisms can flow from the relationships and the idea-generating and norm-deepening functions of such networks. Their importance should not be underestimated.

CHAPTER FOUR

U.S. Approach to the International Order

U.S. Visions of the International Order

As suggested in Chapter Two, U.S. grand strategy since 1945 has linked the promotion of order and the preservation of U.S. national interests in a tight, mutually reinforcing strategic concept. Building an international order has been a formal program of U.S. foreign policy since at least the 1940s and an aspirational goal since the nation's founding.[1] At first, the concept relied on America serving as a model for the world, a vision that imagined the long-term possibility of a community of like-minded nations. After 1939, the U.S. interest in order became more urgent, practical, and intentional. The United States needed to use its newfound power, President Franklin D. Roosevelt and others believed, to ensure that the forces of anarchy and instability that helped lead to war in the 1930s were kept at bay (Weiss, 2015).

From 1945 onward, the United States has integrated the idea of an increasingly structured international order into its national security strategies. Thanks to these U.S. efforts, the postwar decades saw the rise of an "inexorably expanding cooperative order of states observ-

---

[1] In a defining study of the World War II and postwar U.S. embrace of order, Patrick (2009, p. xi) explains,

> Suddenly during World War II the United States heeded an internationalist vocation, assumed global leadership, and sponsored an array of multilateral institutions and partnerships to govern international security, political and economic relations. . . . The goal of this effort was to create an *open world*—a rule-based global order in which peace-loving countries could cooperate to advance their common purposes within international institutions.

ing common rules and norms, embracing common economic systems, forswearing territorial conquest, respecting national sovereignty, and adopting participatory and democratic systems of governance" (Kissinger, 2014, p. 1). With the end of the Cold War, there was hope that this global order would grow beyond its Western core to cover the entire world, and this became a central theme of U.S. national security strategies.

The U.S. search for order encompasses two distinct themes, which flow from the basic philosophies of order described in Chapter Three. Order can be a function of power—order as imposed by a hegemonic state, for example—and it can be a function of mutually agreed rules or constructed norms that reflect shared interests and values. The U.S. approach to order has employed both of these approaches,[2] and the result has been an overarching strategy shot through with dilemmas. At times, the United States has deployed power in ways that have contradicted existing rules and norms, and at other times, it has enunciated rules and norms that have threatened the credible application of its power.

It is when these two approaches have reinforced one another—where power, interests, rules, and norms could work in harmony—that the U.S. effort to build ordering mechanisms has arguably been most effective. The next section lays out the detailed ways in which U.S. national security strategies have discussed and employed the concept of order; all of them make strong reference to the mutually reinforcing aspect of power on the one hand and rules, norms, and institutions on the other. Yet this relationship is undergoing changes on many fronts, including the character and decisiveness of the power being applied, the willingness of leading states to follow rules and norms, and those states' demands to shape and set those rules themselves.

---

[2]   Kissinger (2014, p. 9) writes that any system of order "bases itself on two components: a set of commonly accepted rules that define the limits of permissive action and a balance of power that enforces restraint where rules break down."

The International Order in U.S. National Security Strategy Documents

This section identifies the core elements and institutions of the international order and common themes in U.S. perceptions of the international order as depicted in U.S. National Security Strategy (NSS) documents and selected strategy and policy documents predating the inception of the NSS. Given the differing foreign policy approaches of recent presidential administrations, the lack of variation in the characterization of the international order across NSS documents is surprising. Since their inception in 1987, nearly all NSS documents—as well as NSC-68—reference several themes regarding the maintenance and evolution of the international order. Each NSS refers explicitly to the following four components, which constitute the core elements of the postwar international order:

- a rules-based free trade system
- strong alliances and sufficient military capabilities for effective deterrence
- multilateral cooperation/international law to solve truly global problems, such as the nonproliferation of weapons of mass destruction[3]
- the spread of democracy.

These elements are supported and promoted by a variety of international and regional institutions, including

- economic institutions, led by the WTO (and GATT), regional and bilateral free trade agreements, the IMF and World Bank, and newer groupings of leading nations (such as the Group of Eight and G-20)
- NATO and the global network of regional security order and bilateral alliances (the "hub and spokes" system)

---

[3] See, for example, White House, 1993 (under President Bill Clinton), pp. 16–17; and White House, 2006 (under President George W. Bush), pp. 20, 22.

- international legal treaties and conventions emanating largely from the UN, including the Geneva Conventions, the Non-Proliferation Treaty, and the Chemical Weapons Convention.

Reviewing the history of postwar U.S. national security documents, one finds a continuing, consistent, and powerful commitment to the idea of international order, both as a means to promote specific goals (such as nonproliferation) and, just as important, as an ultimate objective in itself. U.S. postwar grand strategy has been very explicit that the United States seeks a more predictable and peaceful world for its own sake. For a country whose global vision has been transformational since its founding, this should perhaps not come as a surprise. But it raises the question of whether, to what degree, and in what form a transformational approach to order can remain a leading aspect of U.S. national security strategy in a more complex, multipolar era.

U.S. National Security Interests Justify the Existence of International Order

According to its postwar architects, the international order protects U.S. values by maintaining an environment in which the ideals of a free and democratic society—like that of the United States—can flourish. In NSC-68, the authors clearly believed that the Soviet Union and the alternative political and economic system it represented posed the greatest threat to the United States. They also saw that global disorder made this threat particularly potent: If the United States did not bring the weakened nations of the postwar, postcolonial world into an order of its liking, the Soviet Union—with the help of nuclear weapons—could seize the opportunity to create its own opposing order. The following passage from the document is revealing:

> Even if there were no Soviet Union we would face the great problem of the free society, accentuated many fold in this industrial age, of reconciling order, security, the need for participation, with the requirement of freedom. We would face the fact that in a shrinking world *the absence of order among nations is becoming less and less tolerable.* The Kremlin design seeks to impose order among nations by means which would destroy our free and dem-

ocratic system. The Kremlin's possession of atomic weapons puts new power behind its design, and increases the jeopardy to our system. It adds new strains to the uneasy equilibrium-without-order which exists in the world and raises new doubts in men's minds whether the world will long tolerate this tension *without moving toward some kind of order, on somebody's terms.* (Executive Secretary, 1950, p. 34, emphasis added)

Self-interest demanded that the United States take on "the responsibility of world leadership" by "mak[ing] the attempt, and accept[ing] the risks inherent in it, to bring about order and justice by means consistent with the principles of freedom and democracy" (Executive Secretary, 1950, p. 9). This U.S.-led international order would find legitimacy by insisting that relations between nations must occur "on the basis of equality and respect for the rights of others"; in other words, it would "seek to create a world society based on the principle of consent" (Executive Secretary, 1950, p. 9). The themes of U.S. leadership, democracy promotion, and the importance of consent as opposed to coercion will be explored in subsequent sections; the main point here is that the international order was imagined as a critical means of protecting fundamental U.S. values and interests.

The same theme has been woven through all subsequent major statements of U.S. national security strategy, from Republican and Democratic administrations, both during the Cold War and afterward. In national security strategies, national military strategies, and other statements of U.S. grand strategic intent, successive U.S. administrations have returned again and again to the relationship between U.S. power and interests and the international order. They have done this with reference to several themes, including deterring and limiting the use of force, spreading democracy, and enforcing rules and norms.

Consent and Coercion: Deterrence and Limitations on the Use of Force

A central theme in U.S. official treatments of international order is the idea that the use of force is not the best means for achieving and securing U.S. interests. There are two reasons for this. First, for a free society, war must be viewed as a "last resort" because it is the "negation of freedom"; force can be used only to "enforce the rights common to all" (Executive Secretary, 1950, p. 11). Ultimately, war cannot end the "fundamental conflict in the realm of ideas" between democratic and authoritarian forces (p. 11). Instead, the only way to end that conflict is by "demonstrat[ing] the superiority of the idea of freedom" (p. 11) by creating and "maintaining the material environment in which [the values of a free society] flourish" (p. 9). In this view, military power is useful primarily in deterring an attack on the United States, although it may be necessary to fight "to defend the integrity and vitality of our free society" (p. 6). Second, and more practically, obtaining consent to abide by international rules and norms that reinforce U.S. interests is a more efficient and less costly mechanism for achieving cooperation than coercion.

All NSS documents stress the belief that conflict is easiest to stop if it is prevented entirely. For example, the Clinton administration noted the cost savings that result from conflict prevention: "Whenever possible, we seek to avert such humanitarian disasters through diplomacy and cooperation with a wide range of partners, including other governments, international institutions, and nongovernmental organizations. By doing so, we may not only save lives but also prevent the drain on resources caused by intervention in a full-blown crisis" (White House, 1997, p. 11). In spite of this emphasis on deterrence, however, nearly every presidential administration in the postwar era has intervened militarily in selected conflicts around the world where U.S. national interests, broadly conceived, were deemed to be at stake. George H. W. Bush intervened in Kuwait; Clinton intervened in Haiti, Somalia, and Bosnia; the younger Bush intervened in Iraq and Afghanistan; and Obama intervened in Libya. This record suggests that the international order must work—if it does at all—not merely through the logic of deterrence but through punishment of rule violators.

The Spread of Democracy and a Zone of Peace

The ideas that the spread of democracy is good—even essential—for U.S. interests and that it is a central component of any truly sustainable order appear throughout these national security documents. The notion of "making the world safe for democracy" is pervasive. In fact, as mentioned earlier, NSC-68 described the motivation for creating an international order as "creat[ing] the conditions under which our free and democratic system can live and prosper" (Executive Secretary, 1950, p. 5) and "maintaining the material environment in which [the fundamental values of a free society] flourish" (p. 9). Each presidential administration has echoed these terms, affirming the centrality of democratic values to the type of international order that the United States has championed.

There are a few reasons why the spread of democracy is deemed so important. First, democracy is equated with U.S. survival; in other words, it is the fundamental national interest in need of protection (and which the order is designed to protect). Take, for example, this passage from the Ronald Reagan administration's 1988 NSS:

> National Security Strategy must start with the values that we as a nation prize. . . . [V]alues such as human dignity, personal freedom, individual rights, the pursuit of happiness, peace and prosperity . . . are the values that lead us to seek an international order that encourages self-determination, democratic institutions, economic development, and human rights. The ultimate purpose of our National Security Strategy is to protect and advance those values. (White House, 1988, p. 3)

Second, democracy is perceived as the foundation of other core objectives of the order, particularly economic growth and sustainable peace. In 1990, the Bush administration vowed to "promote the growth of free, democratic political institutions, as the surest guarantee of both human rights and economic and social progress" (White House, 1990, p. 3). The Clinton administration explicitly connected the spread of democracy to U.S. security and economic interests, arguing that "democratic governments are more likely to cooperate with each other against common threats and to encourage free and open trade and economic development—and less likely to wage war or abuse the rights of their people" (White House, 1997, p. 5).

In line with "democratic peace theory," the Clinton administration argued that the U.S. security umbrella had provided stability that "nurtured a democratic community of nations—a 'zone of peace' among the Western Hemisphere, Western Europe, and Japan, Australia and the newly industrializing economies of East Asia" (White House, 1993, p. 5). In order to achieve "real peace— . . . an enduring democratic peace based on shared values . . . and the rule of law," the NSS document asserts, the United States should "foster open and democratic systems that secure human rights and respect for every citizen, and work to strengthen respect for international norms of conduct" (White House, 1993, p. 3). Democracy and a stable, rules-based order, in this conception, are inseparable.

The third reason why the spread of democracy is perceived as important for international order builds on this insight: Democratic states are believed to behave more responsibly in their international relations. They are more likely to abide by international norms or to resolve disputes through peaceful bilateral or multilateral mechanisms instead of resorting to war. In 2006, the Bush administration argued that "the goal of our statecraft is to help create a world of democratic, well-governed states that can meet the needs of their citizens and conduct themselves responsibly in the international system" (White House, 2006, p. 1).

The behavior of democracies and the standards embodied in international institutions are portrayed as mutually reinforcing. As the Clinton administration wrote in 1997,

> Working through multilateral institutions, the United States promotes universal adherence to international human rights and democratic principles. Our efforts in the United Nations and other organizations are helping to make these principles the governing standards for acceptable international behavior. (White House, 1997, p. 22)

Successive U.S. administrations have repeatedly referred to the liberal democratic character of the desired U.S.-led international order—a theme that has characterized every postwar administration to some degree; the Clinton administration, for example, explicitly embraced a strategy of "engagement and enlargement" (White House, 1995, p. 2–3), and the George W. Bush administration placed democracy promotion at the center of its own strategy (White House, 1990).

But these documents help reveal the causal assumptions underlying the emphasis on the spread of democracy as beneficial or essential for securing U.S. interests and maintaining the existing order.

Norms and Enforcement: How the Order Works

U.S. national security documents also propose theories of how the order works—the mechanisms by which it achieves its effects. One such mechanism commonly raised in U.S. strategy documents is enforcement. States obey the rules or laws that make up the order because they fear what will happen to them if they disobey. With respect to security, enforcement means "that regions critical to our interests must be defended; that the world must respond to straightforward aggression" (White House, 1993, p. 1). With respect to international laws or treaties—for example, the Non-Proliferation Treaty—enforcement means "hold[ing] nations like Iran and North Korea accountable for their failure to meet international obligations" (White House, 2010, p. 4).

The Obama administration elaborates on this legalistic perspective, explaining that incentives must be aligned with desired behavior (cooperation) and that states must be punished and denied those incentives if they fail to engage in the desired behavior:

> To adversarial governments, we offer a clear choice: abide by international norms, and achieve the political and economic benefits that come with greater integration with the international community; or refuse to accept this pathway, and bear the consequences of that decision, including greater isolation. (White House, 2010, p. 11)

In sum, "nations must have incentives to behave responsibly, or be isolated when they do not" (White House, 2010, p. 12). While the Clinton administration emphasizes the importance of "shaping the international environment to prevent or deter threats" by using "diplomacy, international assistance, arms control programs, nonproliferation initiatives, and overseas military presence" to strengthen alliances and encourage states to abide by international norms (White House, 1997, p. 8), the Obama administration asserts the importance of using sticks in addition to carrots in order to get compliance:

> We will continue to embrace the post-World War II legal archi-
> tecture—from the U.N. Charter to the multilateral treaties that
> govern the conduct of war, respect for human rights, nonprolif-
> eration, and many other topics of global concern—as essential
> to the ordering of a just and peaceful world, where nations live
> peacefully within their borders, and all men and women have the
> opportunity to reach their potential. . . . At the same time, we
> will exact an appropriate cost on transgressors. (White House,
> 2015a, p. 23)

And yet, at the same time, U.S. national security documents
across different administrations have varied in their interpretations of
the extent to which the United States must follow the same rules—
whether it must bind itself to abide by certain international standards
or place itself under the authority of international institutions. The
Obama administration has declared that the United States must lead
by example—which means "holding ourselves to international norms
and standards that we expect other nations to uphold, and admitting
when we do not" (White House, 2010, p. 3). Yet the George W. Bush
administration was equally adamant that the United States should not
be constrained in its foreign policy behavior "by the potential for inves-
tigations, inquiry, or prosecution by the International Criminal Court,
whose jurisdiction does not extend to Americans and which we do
not accept" (White House, 2002, p. 25). These normative questions
have practical implications for U.S. foreign policy and for the maintenance of the order as it exists, but the answers appear indeterminate: If
the most powerful actor is not constrained by the order it has created,
how can the order be sustained as the power dynamics in the international system shift?

U.S. Interests and Approaches to the International Order

U.S. national security statements have identified clear interests and
objectives of U.S. strategy and catalogued numerous ways in which the
liberal, rules-based order can help promote them. In just one example,
in 1997, the Clinton administration described the contours and major

objectives of the international order. The NSS argued, "We seek to create conditions in the world where our interests are rarely threatened, and when they are, we have effective means of addressing those threats" (White House, 1997, p. 6). Specifically, the document suggested that an international order that limits threats to U.S. interests would be one in which

- "no critical region is dominated by a power hostile to the United States and regions of greatest importance to the U.S. are stable and at peace"
- "the global economy and open trade are growing"
- "democratic norms and respect for human rights are increasingly accepted"
- "terrorism, drug trafficking and international crime do not undermine stability and peaceful relations"
- "the spread of nuclear, chemical, biological and other potentially destabilizing technologies is minimized"
- "the international community is willing and able to prevent or respond to calamitous events." (White House, 1997, p. 6)

In service of these core interests, U.S. strategy has employed several approaches. It seeks to *manage great power relations* by creating institutions, habits, practices, norms, and implicit or explicit rules that regulate competition and behavior and provide regularized avenues for cooperation. It aims to *promote global economic stability and development* through a set of institutions, treaties, and rules that promote growth, trade, and regulated exchanges and that provide relief in case of crisis. It attempts to *limit, control, and end conflict and violence* through alliances, institutions, norms, rules, and networks that discourage and constrain conflict. It works to *facilitate multilateral collaboration on shared challenges* through institutions and networks that reduce transaction costs, create regularized pathways for cooperation, and, in other ways, allow collective action. And it tries to *promote liberal institutions, values, and norms* by creating a system of expectations and habits backed by institutions and networks that promote liberal outcomes.

The key question is the degree to which these order-based elements have played an important, marginal, or unimportant role in promoting these interests. The United States could theoretically use other means to promote its interests; some doubt whether the order has achieved much independent of U.S. power (Schweller, 2001). The question is almost impossible to answer in any measurable way because there are too many variables—including relative U.S. power and the role of nuclear weapons—at work on outcomes and behavior to isolate specific effects of the postwar order. Other parts of this study, however, will attempt to examine specific components of the order to make at least a qualitative judgment about their outcomes and relative value.

Conclusion and Policy Implications

Although there have been differences across administrations, the following themes have been constant in U.S. thinking for the past 70 years:[4]

1. *The United States has seen the creation and maintenance of the international order as an important way to promote U.S. interests in the face of a variety of strategic, economic, and global problems.* Order has been envisioned as a means of stemming the tide of Communism (Executive Secretary, 1950), establishing a modus vivendi with the Soviet Union through détente (Gaddis, 1982, p. 289), managing the post–Cold War world (White House, 1991),[5] and sustaining American interests into the 21st century as new powers rise (see White House, 2010, p. 12). Although there was substantial debate about exactly what type of order could best achieve these aims in the years after World War II, U.S. policymakers believed that national security demanded a more active role for the United States in ensuring stability

---

[4] For a similar argument on the continuities in U.S. grand strategy, see Posen, 2014.

[5] According to the 1991 NSS, "A new world order is not a fact; it is an aspiration—and an opportunity. We have within our grasp an extraordinary possibility that few generations have enjoyed—to build a new international system in accordance with our own values and ideals, as old patterns and certainties crumble around us" (White House, 1991, p. v).

among great powers.[6] Going forward, this is one of the most important questions for U.S. policy: Just how necessary is the postwar order to the achievement of U.S. interests? Could it obtain roughly the same results in more unilateral, bilateral, or ad hoc ways? Part of the answer depends on the general perspective of U.S. national security strategy. If it remains fundamentally transformational in outlook, envisioning a future that is more orderly, democratic, and rule-bound, then building on current elements of order is a necessary approach.

2. *U.S. leadership of the order has been seen as both necessary for creating and sustaining the order and desirable for ensuring that the order fulfills U.S. interests.* At the end of World War II, the United States found that U.S. leadership was needed to generate effective collective action (Ikenberry, 2001, pp. 191–199). This fundamental belief in the necessity of U.S. leadership of the international order persisted after the Cold War. U.S. policymakers also feared that U.S. interests would be undermined if another state took up the mantle of leadership. NSC-68, for example, warned that the demand for order in the international system meant that there would eventually be "some kind of order, on somebody's terms" (Executive Secretary, 1950, p. 34). More recently, the Obama administration argued in favor of the Trans-Pacific Partnership by saying, "we can't let countries like China write the rules of the global economy. We should write those rules" (White House, 2015b).

3. *The United States has seen a community of free-market democracies as the core of the international order.* U.S. leaders have consistently argued that such states are more peaceful toward one another. As a result, one way the United States has sought to strengthen the order is by encouraging states to democratize, liberalize, and integrate into shared institutions. The prototypical example is

---

[6] After World War I, there had been greater domestic opposition to President Woodrow Wilson's order-building agenda. Although there were disagreements about the exact form that the order should take after World War II, there was widespread agreement that some order had to be built. See Ikenberry, 2001, pp. 148–155, 175–185; and Executive Secretary, 1950. For a post–Cold War view, see White House, 1997.

the post–Cold War U.S. policy of bringing former Warsaw Pact and Soviet Republics into NATO and supporting their entry into the European Union.

4. *The United States has looked for ways to strengthen the order with states outside of the democratic community.* During World War II, for example, the United States discussed alternative orders that included the Soviet Union, including Roosevelt's "Four Policemen" idea.[7] In later years, President Richard Nixon's strategy of "détente" sought "to change the Soviet Union's concept of international relations, to integrate it as a stable element into the existing world order, and to build on the resulting equilibrium a 'structure of peace' that would end once and for all that persistent abnormality known as the 'Cold War'" (Gaddis, 1982, p. 289). The development of the Non-Proliferation Treaty, arms control treaties, and other agreements during the Cold War provide additional examples of the U.S. interest in order-building outside of the democratic core.

---

[7]   Roosevelt envisioned the four major Allied countries in World War II—the United States, the United Kingdom, the Soviet Union, and the Republic of China—acting as the enforcers of order in their respective spheres of influence. Traces of this idea remain in the five permanent members of the United Nations Security Council.

CHAPTER FIVE

Implications for a Research Agenda

Our project is only just under way, but our research and dialogues so far point to one critical overarching question that has received little attention: What *type* of order should the United States seek over the coming decade? The answer is often taken for granted because American analysts and policymakers have a firm image in their head of "international order" as the liberal internationalist variety pushed by the United States since 1945. But order comes in many flavors, and it is not clear that the dominant model of the past 60 or 70 years can or should be the default approach going forward. In order to develop good strategy and policy, it will be especially important to take seriously the tensions, contradictions, and dilemmas that exist among and between different visions of order.

Arguably, the dominant question for U.S. national security strategy over the coming decade begs an answer to this most fundamental of questions: What sort of world does our strategy seek? After seven decades of building an international order in its image, the United States can probably no longer separate the problem of order from the challenge of grand strategy.

These findings point to the following leading questions for further research—questions that must inform U.S. policy toward international order:

1. What forms of order are most important to U.S. interests and international stability?
2. How effective has the postwar order been at promoting U.S. interests, as well as its larger goals?

3. Is the order healthy, and how would we know?

4. What are other states' policies and perspectives toward the order, and what are the right criteria to measure or evaluate them?

5. Where are the most important areas of alignment, and contestation, between and among the great powers on elements of order?

6. Just what is U.S. strategy trying to preserve, and against what? What should be the focus of U.S. policy? In particular, is the "liberal" character of the current order indispensable?

7. What are the major options for joining order and U.S. grand strategy?

8. What policies could the United States adopt in service of the different options?

Future elements of the study will address each of these questions, with the goal of providing insight to U.S. policymakers in their approach to order.

References

"At the 27th Collective Study Session of the CCP Political Bureau; Xi Jinping Stresses the Need to Push Forward the System of Global Governance," *Xinhua*, October 13, 2015.

Axelrod, Robert, and Robert O. Keohane, "Achieving Cooperation Under Anarchy: Strategies and Institutions," in Kenneth A. Oye, ed., *Cooperation Under Anarchy*, Princeton, N.J.: Princeton University Press, 1986, p. 226–254.

Betts, Richard K., "Institutional Imperialism," *National Interest*, No. 113, June 2011, p. 85.

Bhagwati, Jagdish, *Termites in the Trading System: How Preferential Agreements Undermine Free Trade*, New York: Oxford University Press, 2008.

Buckley, Chris, "China Takes Aim at Western Ideas," *New York Times*, August 19, 2013. As of June 6, 2016:
http://www.nytimes.com/2013/08/20/world/asia/
chinas-new-leadership-takes-hard-line-in-secret-memo.html

Bull, Hedley, *The Anarchical Society: A Study of Order in World Politics*, New York: Columbia University Press, 1977.

Buzan, Barry, "From International System to International Society: Structural Realism and Regime Theory Meet the English School," *International Organization*, Vol. 47, No. 3, 1993, pp. 327–352.

Carin, Barry, Richard Higgott, Jan Aart Scholte, Gordon Smith, and Diane Stone, "Global Governance: Looking Ahead, 2006–2010," *Global Governance*, Vol. 12, No. 1, January–March 2006, pp. 1–6.

Chorev, Nitsan, and Sarah Babb, "The Crisis of Neoliberalism and the Future of International Institutions: A Comparison of the IMF and the WTO," *Theory and Society*, Vol. 38, No. 5, September 2009, pp. 459–484.

Cortell, Andrew P., and James W. Davis, Jr., "How Do International Institutions Matter? The Domestic Impact of International Rules and Norms," *International Studies Quarterly*, Vol. 40, No. 4, 1996, pp. 451–478.

Crocker, Chester A., "The Strategic Dilemma of a World Adrift," *Survival*, Vol. 57, No. 1, February–March 2015, pp. 7–30.

Doyle, Michael, "Kant, Liberal Legacies, and Foreign Affairs," *Philosophy and Public Affairs*, Vol. 12, No. 3, Summer 1983, pp. 205–235.

———, "A Liberal View: Preserving and Expanding the Liberal Pacific Union," in T. V. Paul and John A. Hall, eds., *International Order and the Future of World Politics*, Cambridge, UK: Cambridge University Press, 1999, pp. 19–40.

Elrod, Richard B., "The Concert of Europe: A Fresh Look at an International System," *World Politics*, Vol. 28, No. 2, January 1976, pp. 159–174.

Executive Secretary, "A Report to the National Security Council on United States Objectives and Programs for National Security," National Security Council Report 68, Washington, D.C., April 14, 1950. As of December 16, 2015: https://www.trumanlibrary.org/whistlestop/study_collections/coldwar/documents/pdf/10-1.pdf

Finnemore, Martha, "International Organizations as Teachers of Norms: The United Nations Educational, Scientific, and Cultural Organization and Science Policy," *International Organization*, Vol. 47, No. 4, November 1993, pp. 565–597.

Florini, Ann, "The Evolution of International Norms," *International Studies Quarterly*, Vol. 40, No. 3, September 1996, pp. 363–389.

Gaddis, John Lewis, *Strategies of Containment: A Critical Appraisal of Postwar American National Security Policy*, New York: Oxford University Press, 1982.

Goldgeier, James M., and Michael McFaul, *Power and Purpose: U.S. Policy Toward Russia After the Cold War*, Washington, D.C.: Brookings Institution Press, 2003.

Haass, Richard N., "The Unraveling: How to Respond to a Disordered World," *Foreign Affairs*, Vol. 93, No. 6, November–December 2014, p. 70.

Haggard, Stephen, and Beth A. Simmons, "Theories of International Regimes," *International Organization*, Vol. 41, No. 3, Summer 1987, pp. 491–517.

Harris, Peter, "Losing the International Order: Westphalia, Liberalism and Current World Crises," *The National Interest*, November 2015. As of June 6, 2016: http://nationalinterest.org/feature/losing-the-international-order-westphalia-liberalism-current-14298

Hasenclever, Andreas, and Brigitte Weiffen, "International Institutions Are the Key: A New Perspective on the Democratic Peace," *Review of International Studies*, Vol. 32, No. 4, October 2006, pp. 563–585.

Hawkins, Darren, "Explaining Costly International Institutions: Persuasion and Enforceable Human Rights Norms," *International Studies Quarterly*, Vol. 48, No. 4, December 2004, pp. 779–804.

Hill, Fiona, and Clifford G. Gaddy, *Mr. Putin: Operative in the Kremlin*, Washington, D.C.: Brookings Institution Press, 2013.

Ikenberry, G. John, "Liberal Hegemony and the Future of American Postwar Order," in T. V. Paul and John A. Hall, eds., *International Order and the Future of World Politics*, Cambridge, UK: Cambridge University Press, 1999.

———, *After Victory: Institutions, Strategic Restraint, and the Rebuilding of Order After Major Wars*, Princeton, N.J.: Princeton University Press, 2001.

———, *Liberal Leviathan: The Origins, Crisis, and Transformation of the American World Order*, Princeton, N.J.: Princeton University Press, 2011.

———, "The Future of the Liberal World Order," *Foreign Affairs*, Vol. 90, No. 3, May–June 2011, p. 56. As of September 29, 2015: https://www.foreignaffairs.com/articles/2011-05-01/future-liberal-world-order

Ikenberry, G. John, and Charles A. Kupchan, "Socialization and Hegemonic Power," *International Organization*, Vol. 44, No. 3, Summer 1990, pp. 283–315.

Jervis, Robert, "From Balance to Concert: A Study of International Security Cooperation," in Kenneth A. Oye, ed., *Cooperation Under Anarchy*, Princeton, N.J.: Princeton University Press, 1986, p. 58–79.

Jones, Bruce, and Thomas Wright, "The State of the International Order," Brookings Institution Policy Paper, No. 33, February 2014.

Keck, Margaret E., and Kathryn Sikkink, "Transnational Advocacy Networks in International and Regional Politics," *International Social Science Journal*, Vol. 51, No. 159, 1999, pp. 89–101.

Keohane, Robert O., *Power and Governance in a Partially Globalized World*, London: Routledge, 2002.

Kissinger, Henry, *World Order*, New York: Penguin, 2014.

Koh, Harold, "Why Do Nations Obey International Law?" *Yale Law Journal*, Vol. 106, 1996–1997, p. 2599.

Koremenos, Barbara, Charles Lipson, and Duncan Snidal, "The Rational Design of International Institutions," *International Organization*, Vol. 55, No. 4, Autumn 2001, pp. 761–799.

Krasner, Stephen D., "Structural Causes and Regime Consequences: Regimes as Intervening Variables," *International Organization*, Vol. 36, No. 2, Spring 1982, pp. 185–205.

Kupchan, Charles A., "Unpacking Hegemony: The Social Foundations of Hierarchical Order," in G. John Ikenberry, ed., *Power, Order, and Change in World Politics*, Cambridge: Cambridge University Press, 2014, pp. 19–60.

Kydd, Andrew, "Trust, Reassurance and Cooperation," *International Organization*, Vol. 54, No. 2, Spring 2000, pp. 325–357.

Lake, David A., "Dominance and Subordination in World Politics," in G. John Ikenberry, ed., *Power, Order, and Change in World Politics*, Cambridge University Press, 2014, pp. 61–82.

Larson, Deborah Welch, and Alexei Shevchenko, "Status Seekers: Chinese and Russian Responses to U.S. Primacy," *International Security*, Vol. 34, No. 4, Spring 2010, pp. 63–95.

Lindberg, Tod, "Making Sense of the 'International Community,'" Council on Foreign Relations Working Paper, January 2014.

Martin, Lisa, and Beth A. Simmons, "Theories and Empirical Studies of International Institutions," *International Organization*, Vol. 52, No. 4, 1998, pp. 729–757.

Mayeda, Andrew, "Congress Approves IMF Change in Favor of Emerging Markets," *Bloomberg*, December 18, 2015.

Moravcsik, Andrew, "Taking Preferences Seriously: A Liberal Theory of International Politics," *International Organization*, Vol. 51, No. 4, Autumn 1997, pp. 513–553.

Nadelmann, Ethan A., "Global Prohibition Regimes: The Evolution of Norms in International Society," *International Organization*, Vol. 44, No. 4, Autumn 1990, pp. 479–526.

Patrick, Stewart, *The Best Laid Plans: The Origins of American Multilateralism and the Dawn of the Cold War*, Lanham, Md.: Rowman and Littlefield, 2009.

Pevehouse, Jon C., "Democracy from the Outside-In? International Organizations and Democratization," *International Organization*, Vol. 56, No. 3, 2002, pp. 515–549.

Pierson, Paul, "Increasing Returns, Path Dependence, and the Study of Politics," *American Political Science Review*, Vol. 94, No. 2, June 2000, pp. 251–267.

Posen, Barry R., Restraint: *A New Foundation for U.S. Grand Strategy*, Ithaca, N.Y.: Cornell University Press, 2014.

Putin, Vladimir, "Meeting of the Valdai International Discussion Club," Sochi, Russia: Valdai International Discussion Club, October 24, 2014.

Roach, J. Ashley, "Countering Piracy off Somalia: International Law and International Institutions," *The American Journal of International Law*, Vol. 104, No. 3, July 2010, pp. 397–416.

Rose, Gideon, "What Obama Gets Right: Keep Calm and Carry the Liberal Order On," *Foreign Affairs*, Vol. 93, No. 5, September–October 2015, p. 2.

Schroeder, Paul W., "The 19th Century International System: Changes in the Structure," *World Politics*, Vol. 39, No. 1, October 1986, pp. 1–26.

Schweller, Randall L., "The Problem of International Order Revisited," *International Security*, Vol. 26, No. 1, Summer 2001, pp. 161–185.

———, *Maxwell's Demon and the Golden Apple: Global Discord in the New Millennium*, Baltimore: Johns Hopkins University Press, 2014.

Simmons, Beth A., "Treaty Compliance and Violation," *Annual Review of Political Science*, Vol. 13, No. 1, 2010, pp. 273–296.

Snyder, Quddus Z., "Integrating Rising Powers: Liberal Systemic Theory and the Mechanism of Cooperation," *Review of International Studies*, Vol. 39, 2013, pp. 209–231.

Stent, Angela E., *The Limits of Partnership: U.S.-Russian Relations in the Twenty-First Century*, Princeton, N.J.: Princeton University Press, 2015.

Walsh, James I., "National Preferences and International Institutions: Evidence from European Monetary Integration," *International Studies Quarterly*, Vol. 45, No. 1, March 2001, pp. 59–80.

Waltz, Kenneth N., *Theory of International Politics*, Reading, Mass.: Addison-Wesley, 1979.

Weiss, Thomas G., "The United Nations: Before, During and After 1945," *International Affairs*, Vol. 91, No. 6, 2015, pp. 1221–1235.

White House, "National Security Strategy of the United States," Washington, D.C., January 1988.

———, "National Security Strategy of the United States," Washington, D.C., March 1990.

———, "National Security Strategy of the United States," Washington, D.C., 1991.

———, "National Security Strategy of the United States," Washington, D.C., 1993.

———, "A National Security Strategy of Engagement and Enlargement," Washington, D.C., 1995.

———, "A National Security Strategy for a New Century," Washington, D.C., 1997.

———, "National Security Strategy of the United States of America," Washington, D.C., 2002.

———, "National Security Strategy of the United States of America," Washington, D.C., 2006.

———, "National Security Strategy," Washington, D.C., 2010.

———, "National Security Strategy," Washington, D.C., 2015a.

————, "Statement by the President on the Trans-Pacific Partnership," October 5, 2015b. As of March 14, 2016:
https://www.whitehouse.gov/the-press-office/2015/10/05/
statement-president-trans-pacific-partnership

Wilson, Bruce, "Compliance by WTO Members with Adverse WTO Dispute Settlement Rulings: The Record to Date," *Journal of International Economic Law*, Vol. 10, No. 2, June 2007, pp. 397–403.

Wilson, Peter, "The English School Meets the Chicago School: The Case for a Grounded Theory of International Institutions," *International Studies Review*, Vol. 14, 2012, pp. 567–590.